Healthy Foods
for Kids

Smoothies, Snacks & More

Healthy Foods for Kids

Smoothies, Snacks & More

Publications International, Ltd.

Favorite Brand Name Recipes at www.fbnr.com

Microwave Cooking: Microwave ovens vary in wattage. Use the cooking times as guidelines and check for doneness before adding more time.

Preparation/Cooking Times: Preparation times are based on the approximate amount of time required to assemble the recipe before cooking, baking, chilling or serving. These times include preparation steps such as measuring, chopping and mixing. The fact that some preparations and cooking can be done simultaneously is taken into account. Preparation of optional ingredients and serving suggestions is not included.

Healthy Foods for Kids

Smoothies, Snacks & More

Smoothies & Shakes

sparkling strawberry float

2 tablespoons pink colored sugar (optional)

2 cups (8 ounces) frozen unsweetened strawberries

1 container (6 ounces) strawberry yogurt

½ cup milk

2 tablespoons honey or sugar

2 scoops strawberry sorbet

2 fresh strawberries (optional)

1. Place sugar in small shallow dish. Wet rims of glasses with damp paper towel; dip into sugar. Place glasses upright to dry.

2. Place frozen strawberries, yogurt, milk and honey in blender container and blend until smooth. Divide between prepared glasses. Top each float with scoop of sorbet. Cut fresh strawberries from tip almost to stem end. Place on rim of glasses, if desired. *Makes 2 servings*

Prep Time: 10 minutes

sparkling strawberry floats

chilling out watermelon soda

- **6 cups cubed, seeded watermelon**
- **¾ cup frozen orange-pineapple or apple juice concentrate, thawed**
- **2 cups sparkling water or club soda**
- **1 cup ice cubes**
- **6 small watermelon wedges**

1. Combine juice concentrate and cubed watermelon in blender container or food processor. Cover and process until smooth. Divide sparkling water and ice cubes among 6 glasses. Pour watermelon mixture over water. Stir to combine.

2. Garnish each with watermelon wedge. *Makes 6 (8-ounce) servings*

Prep Time: 10 minutes

berry-banana breakfast smoothie

- **1 container (8 ounces) berry-flavored yogurt**
- **1 ripe banana, cut into chunks**
- **½ cup milk**

Place all ingredients in blender. Cover; blend until smooth.

Makes about 2 cups

tip The two most basic secrets to healthful eating and life-long weight control are eating a variety of foods every day and controlling portion size. Expose your children to lots of different foods and teach them what a normal serving size really looks like.

jungle juice

....

1 banana
1 cup frozen strawberries
1 container (6 ounces) vanilla low-fat yogurt
2 tablespoons frozen orange juice concentrate
2 tablespoons strawberry syrup
Fresh orange slices (optional)

1. Place banana, strawberries, yogurt and juice concentrate in blender. Blend until smooth, scraping down sides of blender as needed.

2. Evenly drizzle syrup around inside of 2 tall, clear glasses; fill with Jungle Juice. Garnish with orange slices. *Makes 2 servings*

"moo-vin" vanilla milk shake

....

1 pint (2 cups) low-fat vanilla ice cream
½ cup fat-free (skim) milk
½ teaspoon vanilla
⅛ teaspoon colored sprinkles

Combine all ingredients except sprinkles in blender container. Cover; blend until smooth. Pour into 2 small glasses. Top with sprinkles; serve immediately.
Makes 2 servings

pineberry smoothie

....

1 ripe DOLE® Banana, quartered
1 cup DOLE® Pineapple Juice
½ cup nonfat vanilla or plain yogurt
½ cup DOLE® Fresh Frozen Strawberries, Raspberries or Blueberries

Combine all ingredients in blender or food processor container. Blend until thick and smooth. Serve immediately. *Makes 2 servings*

Prep Time: 5 minutes

jungle juice

tofu fruit & veggie smoothie

··

  1 cup frozen pineapple chunks
  ½ cup soft tofu
  ½ cup apple juice
  ½ cup orange juice
  1 container (about 2½ ounces) baby food carrots

Place all ingredients in blender. Cover; process 15 to 30 seconds until smooth, using on/off pulsing action to break up chunks. Pour into glasses; serve immediately.   *Makes 2 (1-cup) servings*

cherry-berry smoothie

··

  1 cup frozen whole unsweetened pitted dark sweet cherries
  1 cup frozen whole unsweetened strawberries
  1 cup cranberry-cherry juice

In blender, purée frozen pitted dark sweet cherries, frozen strawberries and juice, stirring as needed, until smooth.   *Makes 1 (16-ounce) serving*

Note: Frozen pitted dark sweet cherries may be replaced with ¾ cup well-drained canned pitted dark sweet cherries and four ice cubes.

Favorite recipe from *National Cherry Growers & Industries Foundation*

tofu fruit & veggie smoothies

banana split shakes

1 small (6-inch) ripe banana
¼ cup fat-free (skim) milk
5 maraschino cherries, drained
1 tablespoon chocolate syrup
⅛ teaspoon coconut extract
4 cups low-fat chocolate frozen yogurt

1. Combine banana, milk, cherries, chocolate syrup and coconut extract in blender. Cover; blend on HIGH speed until smooth.

2. Add frozen yogurt 1 cup at a time. Cover and pulse on HIGH speed after each addition until smooth and thick. Pour into 4 glasses. Garnish with additional maraschino cherries, if desired.   *Makes 4 servings*

tip For an even lower-fat shake, chop 3 large, peeled bananas. Place in resealable food storage bag and freeze until solid. Blend with milk, cherries, chocolate syrup and coconut extract. It will not be as thick and frosty as a shake with ice cream, but will be lower in calories and fat. (This is a great use for over-ripe bananas).

apple smoothie

··

3 cups Michigan Apple cider or Michigan Apple juice
1 cup vanilla lowfat yogurt
1 package (3.4 ounces) instant vanilla pudding mix
  Apple pie spice (optional)

In small bowl, combine Michigan Apple cider, yogurt and pudding mix. Whisk with wire whisk until smooth. Refrigerate 2 hours before serving. Sprinkle with apple pie spice just before serving, if desired. *Makes 4 servings*

Favorite recipe from **Michigan Apple Committee**

strawberry delights

··

2 cups low-fat strawberry ice cream
1 cup sliced fresh strawberries
⅔ cup fat-free (skim) milk
¼ cup orange juice
⅛ teaspoon ground cinnamon
  Additional fresh fruit
  Mint sprigs

1. Place ice cream, strawberries, milk, orange juice and cinnamon in blender or food processor. Blend at high speed until smooth.

2. Pour into glasses. Garnish with additional fruit and mint sprigs, if desired.
Makes 4 servings

chocolate-blueberry soy shake

....

5 ounces (½ cup plus 2 tablespoons) soy milk
2 tablespoons frozen or fresh blueberries (about 20 berries)
¼ teaspoon unsweetened cocoa powder
¼ cup crushed ice

Place all ingredients in blender; blend at high speed 30 seconds or until well blended. Pour into chilled glass to serve.   *Makes 1 serving*

glorious morning smoothie

....

1 cup frozen strawberries
1 cup Fat Free French Vanilla STONYFIELD FARM® Yogurt
1 cup orange juice
3 tablespoons wheat germ

Place ingredients into blender and mix on high speed until smooth. Garnish with a fresh strawberry.   *Makes 2 tall smoothies*

smooth mango shake

....

2 medium very ripe mangoes,* peeled, pitted and sliced
1½ cups fat-free (skim) milk
1 cup vanilla fat-free ice cream or frozen yogurt
3 to 4 teaspoons lime juice
¼ teaspoon ground mace

Very ripe mangoes are essential for the flavor in this shake.

Combine mangoes and milk in food processor or blender; process until well blended. Add ice cream, lime juice and mace; process until smooth. Pour into tall glasses to serve.   *Makes 4 servings*

peachy chocolate yogurt shake

⅔ cup peeled fresh peach slices *or* 1 package (10 ounces) frozen peach
   slices, thawed and drained
¼ teaspoon almond extract
 2 cups (1 pint) vanilla nonfat frozen yogurt
¼ cup HERSHEY'S Syrup
¼ cup nonfat milk

1. Place peaches and almond extract in blender container. Cover; blend until smooth.

2. Add frozen yogurt, syrup and milk. Cover; blend until smooth. Serve immediately.   *Makes 4 servings*

orange smoothies

1 cup fat-free vanilla ice cream or frozen yogurt
¾ cup low-fat (1%) milk
¼ cup frozen orange juice concentrate

1. Combine ice cream, milk and juice concentrate in food processor or blender. Cover; process on high until smooth.

2. Pour mixture into 2 glasses. Serve immediately.   *Makes 2 servings*

peachy chocolate yogurt shakes

frozen florida monkey malts

....

2 bananas, peeled
1 cup milk
5 tablespoons frozen orange juice concentrate
3 tablespoons malted milk powder

1. Wrap bananas in plastic wrap; freeze until solid.

2. Break bananas into pieces; place in blender with milk, juice concentrate and malted milk powder. Blend until smooth; pour into 2 glasses and serve immediately.   *Makes 2 servings*

Prep Time: 5 minutes

red raspberry smoothie

....

⅔ cup frozen raspberries, partially thawed*
½ cup milk
½ cup vanilla frozen yogurt
¼ teaspoon vanilla
   Whole raspberries (optional)

To partially thaw raspberries, place them in a small bowl and microwave on LOW for 1 minute.

1. Place partially thawed raspberries and milk in blender. Cover; process 10 to 15 seconds. Strain mixture through sieve into small bowl to remove seeds. Return strained mixture to blender.

2. Add frozen yogurt and vanilla to blender; process 10 to 15 seconds or until mixture is smooth. Garnish with raspberries.   *Makes 1 (1-cup) serving*

frozen florida monkey malt

berry soy-cream blend

....

2 cups frozen mixed berries
1 can (14 ounces) blackberries, with juice
1 cup soy milk or almond milk
1 cup apple juice
½ cup (4 ounces) soft tofu enriched with calcium

Place all ingredients in blender. Cover; blend on HIGH speed until smooth.
Divide between 2 glasses; serve immediately.   *Makes 2 servings*

tip If your child is allergic to dairy products, they'll
love the thick creamy texture and sweet fruity
flavors of this berry shake. Tofu is high in protein and good for
growing children.

honey lemonade with frozen fruit cubes

....

1½ cups lemon juice
¾ cup honey
9 cups water
48 small pieces assorted fruit

Combine lemon juice and honey in large pitcher; stir until honey is dissolved. Stir
in water. Place 1 to 2 pieces of fruit in each compartment of 2 ice cube trays. Fill
each compartment with honey lemonade and freeze until firm. Chill remaining
lemonade. To serve, divide frozen fruit cubes between tall glasses and fill with
remaining lemonade.   *Makes 9 cups*

Favorite recipe from **National Honey Board**

berry soy-cream blend

quick apple punch

4 cups MOTT'S® Apple Juice
2 cups cranberry juice cocktail
2 tablespoons lemon juice
1 liter ginger ale, chilled
   Crushed ice, as needed

In large bowl, combine apple juice, cranberry juice and lemon juice. Fifteen minutes before serving, add ginger ale and crushed ice. Do not stir.

Makes 15 servings

o.j. yogurt shake

1 cup 2% low-fat milk
1 container (8 ounces) plain or vanilla low-fat yogurt
1 can (6 ounces) frozen orange juice concentrate
2 cups ice cubes, cracked

Add milk, yogurt and orange juice concentrate to food processor or blender. Process until smooth and frothy. Add ice; process until smooth and frothy.

Makes 5 (1-cup) servings

Favorite recipe from *Wisconsin Milk Marketing Board*

quick apple punch

cherry chocolate frosty

1 container (6 ounces) chocolate yogurt
½ cup frozen dark sweet cherries
⅛ to ¼ teaspoon almond extract

1. Combine all ingredients in blender container. Cover; blend on high speed 15 to 30 seconds until smooth.

2. Pour into glass; serve immediately.   *Makes 1 (¾-cup) serving*

"lemon float" punch

Juice of 10 to 12 SUNKIST® lemons (2 cups)
¾ cup sugar
4 cups water
1 bottle (2 liters) ginger ale, chilled
1 pint lemon sherbet or frozen vanilla yogurt
Lemon half-cartwheel slices and fresh mint leaves for garnish

Combine lemon juice and sugar; stir to dissolve sugar. Add water; chill. To serve, in large punch bowl, combine lemon mixture and ginger ale. Add small scoops of sherbet, lemon slices and mint.

Makes about 15 cups (thirty 6-ounce servings)

cherry chocolate frosty

banana-pineapple breakfast shake

··

2 cups plain fat-free yogurt
1 can (8 ounces) crushed pineapple in juice, undrained
1 ripe medium banana
2 tablespoons sugar
1 teaspoon vanilla
⅛ teaspoon ground nutmeg
1 cup ice cubes
Fresh pineapple slices (optional)

Place all ingredients in blender. Cover; blend until smooth. Pour into 4 serving glasses. Garnish with pineapple slices. *Makes 4 servings*

Prep Time: 5 minutes

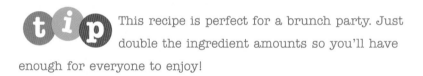 This recipe is perfect for a brunch party. Just double the ingredient amounts so you'll have enough for everyone to enjoy!

raspberry-lemon smoothie

··

1 cup frozen raspberries
1 container (8 ounces) lemon-flavored yogurt
½ cup milk
1 teaspoon vanilla

Place all ingredients in blender. Cover; blend until smooth.

Makes about 1½ cups

banana-pineapple breakfast shake

peanut butter chocolate twist shake

6 ounces frozen vanilla yogurt or ice cream
4 ounces coconut juice or milk
1 ounce chocolate chips
1 ounce peanut butter
2 curls shaved chocolate
½ ounce crushed roasted peanuts

Whip all ingredients except shaved chocolate and peanuts together in blender until smooth. Garnish with shaved chocolate and crushed roasted peanuts.

Makes 1 serving

Favorite recipe from *Peanut Advisory Board*

raspberry watermelon slush

1 cup frozen raspberries
1 cup watermelon, seeded
1 cup lemon-lime seltzer
1 tablespoon sugar

Combine all ingredients in blender or food processor. Blend thoroughly. Serve immediately.

Makes 2 servings

Favorite recipe from *The Sugar Association, Inc.*

plum slush

6 fresh California plums, halved, pitted and coarsely chopped
1 can (6 ounces) frozen cranberry juice concentrate
20 ice cubes, cracked

Add plums, juice concentrate and ice cubes to food processor or blender. Process until smooth. Serve immediately.

Makes 8 servings

Favorite recipe from *California Tree Fruit Agreement*

luscious cocoa smoothies

• •

¼ cup HERSHEY'S Cocoa
2 tablespoons sugar
3 tablespoons warm water
1 banana, peeled and sliced
1½ cups nonfat milk
2 cups nonfat frozen yogurt

Stir together cocoa and sugar in small bowl. Add water; stir until well blended. Place banana and cocoa mixture in blender container. Cover; blend until smooth. Add milk and frozen yogurt. Cover; blend until smooth. Serve immediately.

Makes 4 servings

power shake

• •

1 ripe, medium DOLE® Banana
¾ cup DOLE® Strawberries
½ cup nonfat vanilla yogurt
¼ cup buttermilk
1 tablespoon wheat germ
2 teaspoons honey

Combine banana, strawberries, yogurt, buttermilk, wheat germ and honey in blender or food processor container. Cover; blend until thick and smooth. Serve immediately.

Makes 2 servings

Prep Time: 10 minutes

purple cow jumped over the moon

. . . .

   3 cups vanilla fat-free frozen yogurt
   1 cup reduced-fat (2%) milk
   ½ cup thawed frozen grape juice concentrate, undiluted
1½ teaspoons lemon juice

Place yogurt, milk, juice concentrate and lemon juice in food processor or blender container; process until smooth. Serve immediately.

Makes 8 (½-cup) servings

Razzmatazz Shake: Place 1 quart vanilla fat-free frozen yogurt, 1 cup vanilla fat-free yogurt and ¼ cup chocolate syrup in food processor or blender container; process until smooth. Pour half of mixture evenly into 12 glasses; top with half can (12 ounces) root beer. Fill glasses equally with remaining yogurt mixture; top with remaining root beer. Makes 12 (⅔-cup) servings.

Sunshine Shake: Place 1 quart vanilla fat-free frozen yogurt, 1⅓ cups orange juice, 1 cup fresh or thawed frozen raspberries and 1 teaspoon sugar in food processor or blender container; process until smooth. Pour into 10 glasses; sprinkle with ground nutmeg. Makes 10 (½-cup) servings.

watermelon smoothie

. . . .

2 cups watermelon, seeded, diced
1 cup lowfat vanilla STONYFIELD FARM® Yogurt
1 cup strawberries, frozen
1 cup peach juice

Combine all ingredients in a blender, and purée until smooth. Serve immediately.

Makes 2 tall glasses

purple cow jumped over the moon

mysterious chocolate mint cooler

· ·

  2 cups milk
¼ cup chocolate syrup
  1 teaspoon peppermint extract
   Crushed ice
   Aerosol whipped topping
   Mint leaves

Combine milk, chocolate syrup and peppermint extract in small pitcher; stir until well blended. Fill 2 glasses with crushed ice. Pour chocolate-mint mixture over ice. Top with whipped topping. Garnish with mint leaves.

Makes about 2 (10-ounce) servings

real old-fashioned lemonade

· ·

   Juice of 6 SUNKIST® lemons (1 cup)
¾ cup sugar, or to taste
  4 cups cold water
  1 SUNKIST® lemon, cut into cartwheel slices
   Ice cubes

In large pitcher, combine lemon juice and sugar; stir to dissolve sugar. Add remaining ingredients; blend well.

Makes about 6 cups

Pink Lemonade: Add a few drops of red food coloring or grenadine syrup.

Honeyed Lemonade: Substitute honey to taste for the sugar.

mysterious chocolate mint coolers

Fun Finger Foods

kid kabobs with cheesy mustard dip

Dip

- 1 container (8 ounces) whipped cream cheese
- ¼ cup milk
- 3 tablespoons *French's*® Spicy Brown Mustard or Honey Mustard
- 2 tablespoons mayonnaise
- 2 tablespoons minced green onions

Kabobs

- ½ pound deli luncheon meat or cooked chicken and turkey, cut into 1-inch cubes
- ½ pound Swiss, Cheddar or Monterey Jack cheese, cut into 1-inch cubes
- 2 cups cut-up assorted vegetables such as broccoli, carrots, peppers, cucumbers and celery
- 16 wooden picks, about 6 inches long

1. Combine ingredients for dip in medium bowl; mix until well blended.

2. To make kabobs, place cubes of meat, cheese and chunks of vegetables on wooden picks.

3. Serve kabobs with dip.   *Makes 8 servings (about 1¼ cups dip)*

Prep Time: 15 minutes

kid kabobs with cheesy mustard dip

corny face

....

   1 corn tortilla
   1 slice provolone cheese *or* 3 tablespoons shredded Cheddar cheese
½ large dill pickle, cut at an angle
   2 slices cucumber
   2 pitted black olives
   2 tablespoons shredded carrot

1. Heat nonstick skillet over medium heat; spray skillet lightly with nonstick cooking spray. Place tortilla in skillet; top with cheese. Heat 1 minute; fold tortilla in half, enclosing cheese.

2. Cook 1 minute per side or until cheese is melted and tortilla is lightly browned. Place tortilla, rounded side down, on serving plate. Place pickle on top of tortilla at center to resemble nose. Place cucumber slices on either sides of pickle. Top with olives to resemble eyes. Arrange carrot shreds over cucumbers to resemble eyebrows. *Makes 1 serving*

tuna 'n' celery sticks

....

   4 ounces cream cheese, softened
   3 tablespoons plain yogurt or mayonnaise
1½ teaspoons dried basil
   1 (7-ounce) STARKIST Flavor Fresh Pouch® Tuna (Albacore or Chunk Light)
½ cup finely grated carrot or zucchini
½ cup finely shredded Cheddar cheese
   2 teaspoons instant minced onion
10 to 12 celery stalks, cleaned and strings removed

In large bowl, mix together cream cheese, yogurt and basil until smooth. Add tuna, carrot, Cheddar cheese and onion; mix well. Spread mixture into celery stalks; cut into fourths. *Makes 40 to 48 servings*

Prep Time: 10 minutes

corny face

one potato, two potato

Nonstick cooking spray
2 medium baking potatoes, cut lengthwise into 4 wedges
Salt (optional)
½ cup plain dry bread crumbs
2 tablespoons grated Parmesan cheese (optional)
1½ teaspoons dried oregano, dill weed, Italian seasoning or paprika
Spicy brown or honey mustard, ketchup or reduced-fat sour cream (optional)

1. Preheat oven to 425°F. Spray baking sheet with cooking spray; set aside.

2. Spray cut sides of potatoes generously with cooking spray; sprinkle lightly with salt, if desired.

3. Combine bread crumbs, Parmesan cheese, if desired, and oregano in shallow dish. Add potatoes; toss lightly until potatoes are generously coated with crumb mixture. Place on prepared baking sheet.

4. Bake about 20 minutes until potatoes are brown and tender. Serve warm with mustard for dipping, if desired. *Makes 4 servings*

Potato Sweets: Omit bread crumbs, Parmesan cheese, oregano and mustard. Substitute sweet potatoes for baking potatoes. Cut and spray potatoes as directed; coat generously with desired amount of cinnamon-sugar. Bake as directed. Serve warm with peach or pineapple preserves or honey mustard for dipping. Makes 4 servings.

green meanies

....

4 green apples
1 cup nut butter (peanut, cashew or almond butter)
Almond slivers

1. Place apple, stem side up, on cutting board. Cut away 2 halves from sides of apple, leaving 1-inch-thick center slice with stem and core. Discard core slice. Cut each half round in half. Then cut each apple quarter into two wedges.* Each apple will yield 8 wedges.

2. Spread 2 teaspoons nut butter on wide edge of apple slice. Top with another crinkled edge apple slice, aligning crinkled edges to resemble jaws. Insert almond slivers to make fangs. *Makes 8 servings*

For best effect, use a crinkle cutter garnishing tool to create a toothy look.

turkey bacon mini wafflewiches

....

1 teaspoon Dijon mustard
1 teaspoon honey
8 frozen mini waffles
2 thin slices deli turkey, cut into strips
2 tablespoons cooked and crumbled bacon or bacon bits
4 teaspoons shredded Cheddar or mozzarella cheese
2 teaspoons butter

1. Mix mustard and honey in small bowl. Spread a ¼ teaspoon mustard mixture onto 4 waffles. Top each waffle with turkey and sprinkle with bacon and cheese. Top with 4 remaining waffles.

2. Melt butter in medium nonstick skillet over medium heat. Cook wafflewiches 3 to 4 minutes on each side, pressing with back of spatula, until cheese melts and waffles are golden. *Makes 2 servings*

green meanies

sammich swirls

. . . .

  1 package (about 11 ounces) refrigerated French bread dough
    Yellow mustard
  4 slices light bologna
  4 slices reduced-fat provolone cheese
  2 teaspoons grated Parmesan cheese

1. Preheat oven to 350°F. Roll out bread dough to 10×12-inch rectangle. Dot with mustard.

2. Arrange bologna and cheese in alternating circles, overlapping edges to cover dough. Roll up lengthwise jelly-roll style; pinch seams to seal. Place dough, seam side down, on baking sheet. Sprinkle with grated Parmesan cheese.

3. Bake 25 to 30 minutes or until puffy and browned. Let cool. Cut into 1-inch-thick slices.   *Makes 10 slices*

golden chicken nuggets

. . . .

  1 envelope LIPTON® RECIPE SECRETS® Golden Onion Soup Mix*
  ½ cup plain dry bread crumbs
  1½ pounds boneless, skinless chicken breasts, cut into 2-inch pieces
  2 tablespoons I CAN'T BELIEVE IT'S NOT BUTTER!® Spread, melted

*Also terrific with LIPTON® RECIPE SECRETS® Onion, Onion Mushroom or Savory Herb with Garlic Soup Mix.

1. Preheat oven to 425°F. In small bowl, combine soup mix and bread crumbs. Dip chicken in bread crumb mixture until evenly coated.

2. On lightly greased cookie sheet, arrange chicken; drizzle with spread.

3. Bake uncovered, 15 minutes or until chicken is thoroughly cooked, turning once.   *Makes 6 servings*

Prep Time: 10 minutes
Cook Time: 15 minutes

sammich swirls

tortellini teasers

....

   Zesty Tomato Sauce (recipe follows)
½ (9-ounce) package refrigerated cheese tortellini
 1 large red or green bell pepper, cut into 1-inch pieces
 2 medium carrots, cut into ½-inch pieces
 1 medium zucchini, cut into ½-inch pieces
12 medium fresh mushrooms
12 cherry tomatoes

1. Prepare Zesty Tomato Sauce; keep warm.

2. Cook tortellini according to package directions; drain.

3. Alternate 1 tortellini and 2 to 3 vegetable pieces on long frilled toothpicks or wooden skewers. Serve with Zesty Tomato Sauce.   *Makes 6 servings*

zesty tomato sauce

 1 can (15 ounces) tomato purée
 2 tablespoons finely chopped onion
 2 tablespoons chopped fresh parsley
 1 teaspoon dried oregano
¼ teaspoon dried thyme
¼ teaspoon salt
⅛ teaspoon black pepper

Combine tomato purée, onion, parsley, oregano and thyme in small saucepan. Heat thoroughly, stirring occasionally. Stir in salt and pepper. Transfer to serving bowl; garnish as desired.

mini cheese burritos

··

    2 (8-inch) fat-free flour tortillas
    ¼ cup canned fat-free refried beans
    ¼ cup chunky salsa
    4 (¾-ounce) reduced-fat Cheddar cheese sticks*

Reduced-fat Cheddar cheese block can be substituted. Cut cheese into 2×¼×¼-inch sticks.

1. Cut tortillas in half. Spread beans over tortilla halves, leaving ½-inch border around all edges. Spoon salsa over beans.

2. Cut cheese sticks crosswise in half; arrange on one side of tortilla. Fold rounded edge of tortilla over cheese; roll up. Place burritos, seam side down, on microwavable dish.

3. Microwave on HIGH 1 to 2 minutes or until cheese is melted. Let stand 1 to 2 minutes before serving. *Makes 4 servings*

fantasy cinnamon applewiches

··

    4 slices raisin bread
    ⅓ cup reduced-fat cream cheese
    ¼ cup finely chopped unpeeled apple
    1 teaspoon sugar
    ⅛ teaspoon ground cinnamon

1. Toast bread. Cut into desired shapes using large cookie cutters.

2. Combine cream cheese and apple in small bowl; spread onto toast shapes.

3. Combine sugar and cinnamon in another small bowl; sprinkle evenly over cream cheese mixture. *Makes 4 servings*

Tip: Get out the cookie cutters any time of the year for this fun treat. Or, create your own fun shapes—be sure to have an adult cut out your requested shape with a serrated knife for best results.

mini cheese burritos

super peanut butter sandwiches

⅔ cup peanut butter
2 tablespoons toasted wheat germ
1 tablespoon honey
8 slices firm-texture whole wheat or multi-grain bread
1 ripe banana, sliced
½ cup cholesterol-free egg substitute *or* 2 eggs, beaten
1 tablespoon grated orange peel
⅓ cup orange juice
1 tablespoon margarine or butter

1. Combine peanut butter, wheat germ and honey in small bowl. Spread evenly on one side of each bread slice.

2. Place banana slices on top of peanut butter mixture on four slices of bread. Top with remaining bread slices, peanut butter side down; lightly press together.

3. Combine egg substitute, orange peel and juice in shallow dish. Dip sandwiches in egg mixture, coating both sides.

4. Melt margarine in large nonstick skillet. Cook sandwiches over medium heat until golden brown, turning once. Serve immediately.   *Makes 4 servings*

Prep Time: 15 minutes

tip A cross between a peanut butter sandwich and french toast, this recipe is sure to please. Try it with apples in place of bananas for a crunch.

super peanut butter sandwich

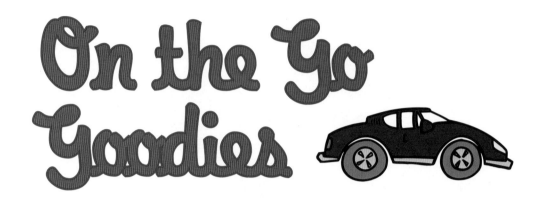

On the Go Goodies

focaccia bars

Cornmeal

1 package (about 11 ounces) refrigerated French bread dough

2 tablespoons olive oil

1 large yellow or red bell pepper, thinly sliced

¼ teaspoon coarse salt

⅛ teaspoon dried oregano

¼ cup shredded Italian cheese blend

1. Preheat oven to 400°F. Sprinkle cornmeal on baking sheet. Shape dough into 16×4-inch rectangle on prepared baking sheet.

2. Heat olive oil in medium skillet over medium-high heat. Add bell pepper; cook and stir 3 to 5 minutes or until pepper is tender and lightly browned. Remove; reserve oil.

3. Press fingertips into dough to create dimples. Drizzle leftover cooking oil from skillet onto dough. Spread pepper slices over dough. Sprinkle with salt and oregano. Top with cheese.

4. Bake 13 to 15 minutes or until cheese melts and bread is golden brown. Let focaccia rest 2 to 3 minutes. Cut into 4 (4-inch) squares. Serve warm or at room temperature. *Makes 4 servings*

Note: Refrigerate leftovers up to two days or freeze up to one month.

focaccia bars

peanut butter-apple wraps

¾ cup creamy peanut butter
4 (7-inch) whole wheat or spinach tortillas
¾ cup finely chopped apple
⅓ cup shredded carrot
⅓ cup low-fat granola without raisins
1 tablespoon toasted wheat germ

Spread peanut butter on one side of each tortilla. Sprinkle each tortilla evenly with apple, carrot, granola and wheat germ. Roll up tightly; cut in half. Serve immediately or refrigerate until ready to serve. *Makes 4 servings*

Prep Time: 5 minutes
Chill Time: 2 hours

spicy fruity popcorn mix

4 cups lightly salted popped popcorn
2 cups corn cereal squares
1½ cups dried pineapple wedges
1 package (6 ounces) dried fruit bits
Butter-flavored cooking spray
2 tablespoons sugar
1 tablespoon ground cinnamon
1 cup yogurt-covered raisins

1. Preheat oven to 350°F. Combine popcorn, cereal, pineapple and fruit bits in large bowl; mix lightly. Transfer to 15×10-inch jelly-roll pan. Spray mixture generously with cooking spray.

2. Combine sugar and cinnamon in small bowl. Sprinkle half of sugar mixture over popcorn mixture; toss lightly to coat. Spray mixture again with additional cooking spray. Add remaining sugar mixture; toss lightly.

3. Bake 10 minutes, stirring after 5 minutes. Cool completely in pan on wire rack. Add raisins; mix lightly. *Makes about 8½ cups snack mix*

peanut butter-apple wraps

chicken nuggets in a pocket

¼ cup milk

1 egg

1 cup cornbread stuffing, crushed into small pieces*

¼ cup grated Parmesan cheese

1 pound boneless skinless chicken breasts, cut into 24 pieces

4 (6-inch) pita bread rounds with pockets, cut in half

1 cup shredded lettuce

¼ to ½ cup reduced-fat ranch dressing or barbecue sauce

Use seasoned packaged cornbread stuffing, not croutons.

1. Preheat oven to 400°F. Grease baking sheet; set aside.

2. Beat milk and egg together in shallow bowl. Combine cornbread stuffing and cheese in shallow pan. Dip chicken into egg mixture, then roll chicken in cornbread mixture. Pat nuggets to help coating adhere.

3. Place chicken on baking sheet. Bake 8 to 10 minutes or until cooked through and golden.

4. To serve, fill each pita half with lettuce. Add 3 chicken nuggets to each half. Drizzle 1 to 2 tablespoons ranch dressing into each pocket.   *Makes 4 servings*

tip To pack for lunch, prepare in advance and chill the chicken. Pack into the pita as directed, wrap and place into insulated lunch bag to keep cool. Spoon ranch dressing into small container with sealable lid. Include a frozen juice box or frozen gel pack. Tell your kids to throw away leftovers.

chicken nuggets in a pocket

tic tac toe sandwich

....

2 teaspoons mayonnaise
1 slice whole wheat bread
1 slice white sandwich bread
1 slice cheese
1 slice deli ham
3 olives, black or green

1. Spread 1 teaspoon mayonnaise on each slice of bread. Layer cheese and ham on one bread slice. Top with remaining slice. Trim crust from bread. Cut sandwich into 9 pieces by cutting into thirds in each direction. Turn alternating pieces over to form checkerboard pattern.

2. Thinly slice 1 olive to form 'O's. Cut remaining 2 olives into strips. Place olive pieces on sandwich squares to form 'X's and 'O's.   *Makes 1 sandwich*

Prep Time: 5 minutes

banana roll-ups

....

¼ cup smooth or crunchy almond butter
2 tablespoons mini chocolate chips
1 to 2 tablespoons milk
1 (8-inch) whole wheat flour tortilla
1 large banana, peeled

1. Combine almond butter, chocolate chips and 1 tablespoon milk in medium microwavable bowl. Microwave on MEDIUM (50%) 40 seconds. Stir well; repeat if necessary to melt chocolate. Add more milk if necessary for desired consistency.

2. Spread almond butter mixture on tortilla. Place banana on one side of tortilla and roll up tightly. Cut into 8 slices.   *Makes 4 servings*

cinnamon toast poppers

···

  2 tablespoons butter
  6 cups fresh bread* cubes (1-inch cubes)
  1 tablespoon plus 1½ teaspoons sugar
  ½ teaspoon ground cinnamon

Use a firm sourdough, whole wheat or semolina bread.

1. Preheat oven to 325°F. Melt butter in Dutch oven or large skillet over low heat. Add bread cubes and toss to coat; remove from heat. Combine sugar and cinnamon in small bowl. Sprinkle over bread cubes; stir well.

2. Spread bread cubes in one layer on ungreased baking sheet. Bake 25 minutes or until bread is golden and fragrant, stirring once or twice. Serve warm or at room temperature.   *Makes 12 servings*

take-along snack mix

···

  1 tablespoon butter or margarine
  2 tablespoons honey
  1 cup toasted oat cereal, any flavor
  ½ cup coarsely broken pecans
  ½ cup thin pretzel sticks, broken in half
  ½ cup raisins
  1 cup "M&M's"® Chocolate Mini Baking Bits

In large heavy skillet over low heat, melt butter. Add honey; stir until blended. Add cereal, nuts, pretzels and raisins; stir until all pieces are evenly coated. Continue cooking over low heat 10 minutes, stirring frequently. Remove from heat; immediately spread on waxed paper until cool. Add "M&M's"® Chocolate Mini Baking Bits. Store in tightly covered container.   *Makes about 3½ cups*

cinnamon toast poppers

ham, apple and cheese turnovers

1¼ cups chopped cooked ham
¾ cup finely chopped red apple
¾ cup (3 ounces) shredded reduced-fat Cheddar cheese
1 tablespoon brown mustard (optional)
1 package (about 14 ounces) refrigerated pizza dough

1. Preheat oven to 400°F. Spray baking sheet with nonstick cooking spray. Combine ham, apple, cheese and mustard, if desired, in medium bowl; set aside.

2. Roll pizza dough into 15×10-inch rectangle on lightly floured surface. Cut into six (5-inch) squares. Top each square evenly with ham mixture. Moisten edges with water. Fold dough over filling. Press edges to seal. Place on prepared baking sheet.

3. Prick tops of each turnover with fork. Bake about 15 minutes or until golden brown. Serve warm or at room temperature. Store leftovers in refrigerator.

Makes 6 servings

Prep Time: 15 minutes
Bake Time: 15 minutes

ham, apple and cheese turnovers

inside-out breadsticks

· ·

   1 package (about 11 ounces) refrigerated breadsticks (12 breadsticks)
   1 package (8 ounces) reduced-fat cream cheese, softened
   1 to 2 tablespoons milk
  ¼ cup finely chopped carrot
   2 tablespoons minced chives or green onion
  12 slices deli ham, roast beef, turkey or chicken

1. Bake breadsticks according to package directions; cool.

2. Beat cream cheese with 1 tablespoon milk, adding additional to make mixture spreadable, if needed. Stir in carrot and chives. Spread 1 rounded tablespoon cream cheese mixture over ham slice. Roll ham slice around breadstick. Repeat with remaining breadsticks. Wrap tightly in plastic wrap. Refrigerate until ready to serve.

Makes 6 servings

Note: Wrap and freeze unused breadsticks. Cream cheese spread may be refrigerated two days.

tip To keep breadsticks cool in a lunchbox, include a frozen juice box or frozen gel pack. Tell your kids to throw away leftovers.

inside-out breadsticks

cinnamon-raisin roll-ups

4 ounces reduced-fat cream cheese, softened
½ cup shredded carrot
¼ cup golden or dark raisins
1 tablespoon honey
¼ teaspoon ground cinnamon
4 (7- to 8-inch) whole wheat or flour tortillas
8 thin apple wedges

1. Combine cream cheese, carrot, raisins, honey and cinnamon in small bowl; mix well.

2. Spread tortillas evenly with cream cheese mixture, leaving ½-inch border around each tortilla edge. Place 2 apple wedges down center of each tortilla; roll up tightly. Wrap in plastic wrap. Refrigerate until ready to serve.

Makes 4 servings

Tip: Make sure that the tortillas are at room temperature when you use them. If tortillas are too cold they might crack, making it difficult to roll.

cinnamon-raisin roll-ups

mysterious colorful jiggles

1 package (4 serving size) lime gelatin
1 package (4 serving size) orange gelatin
1 package (4 serving size) blue raspberry gelatin
    Whipped topping
    Multi-colored sprinkles

1. Prepare lime gelatin according to package directions and place in small pitcher or 2-cup measuring cup. Pour ¼ cup lime gelatin mixture into each serving cup. Refrigerate 1 hour or until gelatin is partially set.

2. Prepare orange gelatin according to package directions and place in small pitcher or 2-cup measuring cup. Pour ¼ cup orange gelatin into cups and refrigerate about 1 hour until partially set.

3. Prepare blue raspberry gelatin according to package directions and place in small pitcher or 2-cup measuring cup. Pour ¼ cup blue raspberry gelatin into cups and refrigerate about 1 hour until firm.

6. Serve with whipped topping and sprinkles.   *Makes 8 servings*

pretty pink pies

....

1 small ripe banana, sliced
1 package (4 ounces) mini graham cracker crumb pie crusts (6 crusts)
2 tablespoons chocolate ice cream topping
2 containers (6 ounces each) strawberry low-fat yogurt
6 miniature pastel marshmallows or miniature marshmallows
6 medium fresh strawberries, cut into wedges

1. Place banana slices into pie crusts. Drizzle each with 1 teaspoon chocolate topping. Spoon yogurt over top.

2. Place 1 marshmallow in the center of each tart. Arrange strawberry pieces around marshmallow to resemble flower. Serve immediately or cover and refrigerate up to 4 hours. *Makes 6 servings*

Prep Time: 10 minutes

monkey parfaits

....

1 banana, sliced
1 container (8 ounces) strawberry yogurt
1 cup seedless red grapes or pitted cherries, halved
½ cup flaked coconut (optional)
½ cup mandarin oranges, drained
4 grapes or pitted cherries

For each parfait, layer one-fourth banana slices, 2 tablespoons yogurt, one-fourth grapes, one-fourth coconut, if desired, and one-fourth oranges in 4 parfait glasses. Top each serving with one whole grape. *Makes 4 servings*

Prep Time: 10 minutes

pretty pink pies

jiggly banana split

. . . .

3 gelatin snack cups (3 ounces each), any flavors
1 banana
3 tablespoons whipped topping
    Colored sprinkles
    Maraschino cherries

1. Unmold snack cups by dipping partially in warm water for a few seconds. Slide gelatin from cups into center of serving dish.

2. Peel banana and cut in half lengthwise. Place banana slices on each side of gelatin.

3. Top with whipped topping, sprinkles and cherries.   *Makes 2 servings*

Prep Time: 5 minutes

chocolate panini bites

. . . .

¼ cup chocolate hazelnut spread
 4 slices sandwich bread or Italian bread

1. Preheat indoor grill.* Spread chocolate hazelnut spread evenly over two slices bread; top with remaining slices.

2. Spray sandwiches lightly with nonstick cooking spray. Grill 2 to 3 minutes or until bread is golden brown. Cut sandwiches into triangles.   *Makes 4 servings*

Panini can also be made on the stove on a ridged grill pan or in a nonstick skillet. Cook sandwiches over medium heat about 2 minutes per side.

Chocolate Raspberry Panini Bites: Spread 2 slices bread with raspberry jam or preserves; spread remaining slices with chocolate hazelnut spread. Cook sandwiches as directed above; watch grill or pan closely because jam burns easily.

jiggly banana split

luau fruit cups

··

1 container (6 ounces) piña colada, lemon or vanilla low-fat yogurt
4 waffle cups or cones
2 cups chopped pineapple, strawberries, mango and green grapes
    Ground nutmeg
2 tablespoons flaked coconut, toasted (optional)

Spoon about one-eighth yogurt into each waffle cups. Top each cup evenly with fruit. Spoon remaining yogurt over fruit. Sprinkle with nutmeg. Top with coconut, if desired. Serve immediately. *Makes 4 servings*

Prep Time: 5 minutes

polar bear banana bites

··

1 medium banana, cut into 6 equal-size pieces
¼ cup creamy peanut butter*
3 tablespoons fat-free (skim) milk
¼ cup miniature marshmallows
2 tablespoons unsalted dry-roasted peanuts, chopped (optional)
1 tablespoon chocolate-flavored sprinkles

Soy butter or almond butter can be used in place of peanut butter.

1. Insert toothpick into each banana piece. Place on tray lined with waxed paper.

2. Whisk together peanut butter and milk. Combine marshmallows, peanuts, if desired, and chocolate sprinkles in shallow dish. Dip each banana piece in peanut butter mixture, allowing excess to drip off. Roll in marshmallow mixture. Place on tray; let stand until set. *Makes 3 servings*

luau fruit cup

cracker toffee

· ·

72 rectangular butter-flavored crackers
1 cup (2 sticks) unsalted butter
1 cup packed brown sugar
¼ teaspoon salt
2½ cups semisweet chocolate chips
2 cups chopped pecans

1. Preheat oven to 375°F. Line 17×12-inch jelly-roll pan with heavy-duty foil. Spray generously with nonstick cooking spray. Arrange crackers with edges touching in pan; set aside.

2. Combine butter, brown sugar and salt in heavy medium saucepan. Heat over medium heat until butter melts, stirring frequently. Increase heat to high; boil 3 minutes without stirring. Pour mixture evenly over crackers; spread to cover.

3. Bake 5 minutes. Immediately sprinkle chocolate chips evenly over crackers; spread to cover. Sprinkle pecans over chocolate, pressing to adhere. Cool to room temperature. Refrigerate 2 hours. Break into chunks to serve.

Makes 24 servings

tip Substitute peanut butter chips for chocolate chips and coarsely chopped, lightly salted peanuts for chopped pecans.

cracker toffee

banana caterpillars

2 medium bananas
¼ cup peanut butter
¼ cup flaked coconut
4 raisins
6 thin pretzel sticks

1. Peel and slice each banana into 10 segments. Assemble "caterpillar" by spreading segments with peanut butter and pressing pieces together.

2. Sprinkle half of coconut over each "caterpillar" and press lightly to coat. Use additional peanut butter to press raisins on one end to form "eyes." Break pretzel sticks into small pieces for "legs" and "antenna." *Makes 2 servings*

Tip: Kids can also be creative and add other types of sliced fruits (strawberries, apples, pears) to their caterpillars.

fun fruit kabobs

4 small strawberries (or 2 large strawberries cut in half lengthwise) with
     green leaves removed
4 banana slices (¼ of small banana)
4 green grapes
4 (2¼-inch) pretzel sticks

Gently push 1 strawberry, 1 banana slice and 1 grape onto each pretzel stick. Twist pretzel as you push fruit onto it to keep from breaking. Serve immediately.
Makes 1 serving

banana caterpillar

Fabulously Frozen

wacky watermelon

4 cups diced seedless watermelon (1-inch cubes)
¼ cup strawberry fruit spread
2 cups fat-free vanilla frozen yogurt
2 tablespoons mini chocolate chips, divided

1. Place 2 cups watermelon and fruit spread in blender. Cover and pulse on low until smooth. Add remaining watermelon; cover and pulse until smooth. Add yogurt, 1 cup at a time, pulsing after each addition until smooth.

2. Pour mixture into medium loaf pan (8×4 inches) and freeze 2 hours or until mixture begins to harden around edge of pan. Stir well until mixture is smooth and slushy. Evenly stir in 1½ tablespoons chocolate chips. Smooth out top of mixture with the back of spoon. Sprinkle evenly with remaining chocolate chips. Cover pan with foil and return to freezer until solid, 6 hours or overnight.

3. To serve, place the pan in warm water briefly; invert onto cutting board. Let stand 5 minutes on cutting board to soften slightly. Cut loaf into slices. Serve immediately.

4. Wrap leftover slices individually in plastic wrap and place upright in clean loaf pan. Store in freezer.

Makes 12 servings

frozen chocolate-covered bananas

· ·

  2 ripe medium bananas
  4 wooden popsicle sticks
  ½ cup low-fat granola cereal without raisins
  ⅓ cup hot fudge topping, at room temperature

1. Line baking sheet with waxed paper; set aside.

2. Peel bananas; cut each in half crosswise. Insert wooden stick 1½ inches into center of cut end of each banana. Place on prepared baking sheet; freeze until firm, at least 2 hours.

3. Place granola in large resealable food storage bag; crush slightly using rolling pin or meat mallet. Transfer granola to shallow plate. Place hot fudge topping in shallow dish.

4. Working with 1 banana at a time, place frozen banana in hot fudge topping; spread evenly onto banana with small rubber scraper. Immediately place banana on plate with granola; turn to lightly coat. Return to baking sheet in freezer. Repeat with remaining bananas.

5. Freeze until hot fudge topping is very firm, at least 2 hours. Let stand 5 minutes before serving. *Makes 4 servings*

sinister slushies

· ·

  4 bottles brightly colored sports drinks
  4 to 8 ice cube trays

1. Pour each sports drink into separate ice cube tray; freeze overnight.

2. Just before serving, place each color ice cubes into separate large resealable food storage bags. Seal bags; crush cubes with rolling pin.

3. Layer different colors ice slush in clear glasses. *Makes 4 to 8 servings*

creamy strawberry-orange pops

1 container (8 ounces) strawberry fat-free yogurt

¾ cup orange juice

2 teaspoons vanilla

2 cups frozen whole strawberries

2 teaspoons sugar

6 (7-ounce) paper cups

6 wooden popsicle sticks

1. Combine yogurt, orange juice and vanilla in food processor or blender. Cover and process until smooth.

2. Add strawberries and sugar. Process until smooth. Pour into paper cups, filling each about three-fourths full. Freeze 1 hour. Insert wooden stick into center of each. Freeze completely. Peel cup off each pop to serve.   *Makes 6 servings*

banana tot pops

3 firm, medium DOLE® Bananas

6 large wooden sticks

½ cup raspberry or other flavored yogurt

1 jar (1¾ ounces) chocolate or rainbow sprinkles

• Cut each banana crosswise in half. Insert wooden stick into each half.

• Pour yogurt into small bowl. Hold banana pop over bowl; spoon yogurt to cover all sides of banana. Allow excess yogurt to drip into bowl. Sprinkle candies over yogurt.

• Place pops on wax paper-lined tray. Freeze 2 hours.   *Makes 6 servings*

Prep Time: 20 minutes
Freeze Time: 2 hours

creamy strawberry-orange pops

frozen apple slushies

....

½ cup frozen unsweetened apple juice concentrate
1 cup 100% cranberry juice, chilled
1 large Red Delicious apple, peeled and cut into chunks
⅛ teaspoon ground cinnamon
3 cups ice cubes

1. Place apple juice concentrate, cranberry juice, apple chunks, and cinnamon into blender container. Cover and blend on HIGH speed until smooth. Add ice cubes, 1 cup at a time; cover and blend after each addition until slushy.

2. Freeze leftovers in 1-cup servings in small airtight microwave-safe containers. To serve, microwave each serving for 15 seconds, then stir. Continue microwaving in 10-second increments until slushy.   *Makes 4 servings*

maraschino-lemonade pops

....

1 (10-ounce) jar maraschino cherries
8 (3-ounce) paper cups
1 (12-ounce) can frozen pink lemonade concentrate, partly thawed
¼ cup water
8 popsicle sticks

Drain cherries, reserving juice. Place one whole cherry in each paper cup. Coarsely chop remaining cherries. Add chopped cherries, lemonade concentrate, water and reserved juice to container of blender or food processor; blend until smooth. Fill paper cups with equal amounts of cherry mixture. Freeze several hours or until very slushy. Place popsicle sticks in the center of each cup. Freeze 1 hour longer or until firm. To serve, peel off paper cups.   *Makes 8 servings*

Note: Serve immediately after peeling off paper cups—these pops melt very quickly.

Favorite recipe from *Cherry Marketing Institute*

triple chocolate cups

....

2 cups low-fat chocolate frozen yogurt
1 cup fat-free (skim) milk
2 tablespoons chocolate syrup
¼ cup crushed chocolate wafer crumbs
   Whipped cream or nondairy whipped topping
   Chocolate sprinkles or decors (optional)

1. Line 24 mini (1¾-inch) muffin pan cups with paper baking cups. Combine yogurt, milk and chocolate syrup in blender; cover. Blend on HIGH speed until smooth. Add chocolate wafer crumbs; cover and pulse on HIGH speed until mixed. Spoon mixture into prepared muffin cups, filling three-fourths full. Freeze 1 hour or until solid.

2. If paper baking cups stick to muffin pan, thaw at room temperature 10 to 15 minutes or until baking cups can be easily removed. Just before serving, garnish with whipped cream and chocolate sprinkles. Freeze leftovers in airtight container.

Makes 24 cups

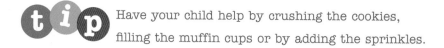 Have your child help by crushing the cookies, filling the muffin cups or by adding the sprinkles.

frozen rainbow bubbler

· ·

1 packet (2-quart size) fruit-flavored powdered drink mix
2 cups water
1 (2-liter) bottle ginger ale, chilled

Dissolve powdered drink mix in water, stirring to mix well. Pour into 1½ ice cube trays (should make about 16 ice cubes, each with about 1 ounce liquid). Freeze until solid. Place 3 ice cubes in a tall glass. Fill glass with ginger ale; stir gently.

Makes 5 servings

Tip: Prepare ice cubes from 2 or more of your favorite flavors of drink mix and combine for an extra layer of flavor. Keep ice cubes sealed in airtight containers or freezer bags until ready to use to avoid picking up flavors from the other foods in your freezer.

berry striped pops

· ·

2 cups strawberries
¾ cup honey,* divided
12 (3-ounce) paper cups or popsicle molds
12 popsicle sticks
6 kiwifruit, peeled and sliced
2 cups sliced peaches

Honey should not be fed to infants under one year of age. Honey is a safe and wholesome food for older children and adults.

Purée strawberries with ¼ cup honey in blender or food processor. Divide mixture evenly between 12 cups or popsicle molds. Freeze about 30 minutes or until firm. Meanwhile, rinse processor; purée kiwifruit with ¼ cup honey. Repeat process with peaches and remaining ¼ cup honey. When strawberry layer is firm, pour kiwifruit purée into molds. Insert popsicle sticks and freeze about 30 minutes or until firm. Pour peach purée into molds and freeze until firm and ready to serve.

Makes 12 servings

Favorite recipe from **National Honey Board**

frozen rainbow bubblers

Acknowledgments

The publisher would like to thank the companies listed below for the use of their recipes in this publication.

California Tree Fruit Agreement

Cherry Marketing Institute

Dole Food Company, Inc.

The Hershey Company

TM/© Mars, Incorporated 2007

Michigan Apple Committee

Mott's® is a registered trademark of Mott's, LLP

National Cherry Growers & Industries Foundation

National Honey Board

Peanut Advisory Board

Reckitt Benckiser Inc.

StarKist® Tuna

Stonyfield Farm®

The Sugar Association, Inc.

Reprinted with permission of Sunkist Growers, Inc. All Rights Reserved.

Unilever

Wisconsin Milk Marketing Board

Metric Chart

VOLUME MEASUREMENTS (dry)

⅛ teaspoon = 0.5 mL
¼ teaspoon = 1 mL
½ teaspoon = 2 mL
¾ teaspoon = 4 mL
1 teaspoon = 5 mL
1 tablespoon = 15 mL
2 tablespoons = 30 mL
¼ cup = 60 mL
⅓ cup = 75 mL
½ cup = 125 mL
⅔ cup = 150 mL
¾ cup = 175 mL
1 cup = 250 mL
2 cups = 1 pint = 500 mL
3 cups = 750 mL
4 cups = 1 quart = 1 L

VOLUME MEASUREMENTS (fluid)

1 fluid ounce (2 tablespoons) = 30 mL
4 fluid ounces (½ cup) = 125 mL
8 fluid ounces (1 cup) = 250 mL
12 fluid ounces (1½ cups) = 375 mL
16 fluid ounces (2 cups) = 500 mL

WEIGHTS (mass)

½ ounce = 15 g
1 ounce = 30 g
3 ounces = 90 g
4 ounces = 120 g
8 ounces = 225 g
10 ounces = 285 g
12 ounces = 360 g
16 ounces = 1 pound = 450 g

DIMENSIONS

1/16 inch = 2 mm
⅛ inch = 3 mm
¼ inch = 6 mm
½ inch = 1.5 cm
¾ inch = 2 cm
1 inch = 2.5 cm

OVEN TEMPERATURES

250°F = 120°C
275°F = 140°C
300°F = 150°C
325°F = 160°C
350°F = 180°C
375°F = 190°C
400°F = 200°C
425°F = 220°C
450°F = 230°C

BAKING PAN SIZES

Utensil	Size in Inches/Quarts	Metric Volume	Size in Centimeters
Baking or Cake Pan (square or rectangular)	8×8×2	2 L	20×20×5
	9×9×2	2.5 L	23×23×5
	12×8×2	3 L	30×20×5
	13×9×2	3.5 L	33×23×5
Loaf Pan	8×4×3	1.5 L	20×10×7
	9×5×3	2 L	23×13×7
Round Layer Cake Pan	8×1½	1.2 L	20×4
	9×1½	1.5 L	23×4
Pie Plate	8×1¼	750 mL	20×3
	9×1¼	1 L	23×3
Baking Dish or Casserole	1 quart	1 L	—
	1½ quart	1.5 L	—
	2 quart	2 L	—